When the Boss is Not Looking

A Book Dealing with Employee Behavior and Work Ethics in the Workplace.

By James E. Puckett

Copyright © 2008 by James E. Puckett

All rights reserved. No part of this book shall be reproduced or transmitted in any form or by any means, electronic, mechanical, magnetic, photographic including photocopying, recording or by any information storage and retrieval system, without prior written permission of the publisher. No patent liability is assumed with respect to the use of the information contained herein. Although every precaution has been taken in the preparation of this book, the publisher and author assume no responsibility for errors or omissions. Neither is any liability assumed for damages resulting from the use of the information contained herein.

ISBN 0-7414-4512-3

Scriptures quotations are from the Kings James Version of the Bible by Thomas Nelson 1990

Published by:

INFINITY
PUBLISHING.COM

1094 New DeHaven Street, Suite 100
West Conshohocken, PA 19428-2713
Info@buybooksontheweb.com
www.buybooksontheweb.com
Toll-free (877) BUY BOOK
Local Phone (610) 941-9999
Fax (610) 941-9959

Printed in the United States of America

Printed on Recycled Paper

Published January 2008

For

When the Boss is Not Looking

TO : _____,

I pray this book will help you on your job and in your career. Thank you for your support. May God continue to bless you.

Author: _____.

Date: _____.

Dedicated to every person who is now working a job or will someday work one.

Contents

Acknowledgments	1
Author's Preface	3
Foreword	5-15
Chapter 1: Your Motive for Working	17
Chapter 2: Work Hard at What You Do	25
Chapter 3: You Are Only as Good as Your Word	31
Chapter 4: When You Feel Your Pay Doesn't Equal Your Labor	36
Chapter 5: Be a Person of Consistency Where You Work	42
Chapter 6: The Boss is "Looking"	49
Conclusion	53
Scriptures Used in the Preparation of this Manuscript	54

Acknowledgments

Special thanks:

To Hallerin Hilton Hill, Dr. Jill Hobby, Mark Roy, Howard III and Tammy Sentell, Marshall Wilkins, Gabriela Gagnier, and J. Craig Smith for your contribution in writing a foreword to this book. I hold each of you to the highest esteem for what you do and for your comments.

To Laura Freeman, a very special friend, for her consultation and editorial work in the preparation of this manuscript. Thank you Laura for being so patient with me.

To Reymund Edrosolano for his remarkable work in the cover design. Reymund, you have set a new standard for yourself.

To my beautiful and lovely wife, Brenda, for listening to all my complaints and concerns as I wrote this book. Thank you for your prayers and continual love and support.

To the Holy Spirit, who lead and directed me in every step of the way in this work.

Author's Preface

Dear Reader,

The core of this book explores and addresses employee work habits and character in the work place. The principles can be applied to any organization or group seeking a common single goal.

In my book for teens, *24/7 Success: Living a Lifetime of Success,* I showed teens and young adults what true success in life is and what it is not. In *When The Boss Is Not Looking,* I want to share with you some of my personal experiences. They highlight principles that are important for every person to practice in the workplace after landing that job in order to achieve true success. This book is for every person who is presently working or seeking that ultimate "dream" job. This book is also for those who are part of an organization seeking a means of building unity among its members in order to achieve a goal. There are lots of people who want titles, but no responsibility.

If you don't like what you are doing, it may be time for you to find another career. Do you really respect your job and what you do on a daily basis? How much do you respect and support your boss? Do you view your job as just a means of receiving a paycheck? If you respect and honor your paycheck more than you respect and honor your job, you have the wrong view for doing what you do. Do you see your job as a dead end? Do you see yourself as not having the potential to be promoted? Maybe it is time that you take a mental examination of yourself and your job. People who feel that they only work for a paycheck will most likely do the least amount of work possible. They will never do more than is required of them, but will always seek to do the minimum. They do not care if the boss is looking or not.

Their minds are made up that their job can only offer so much, and they can only go so far. Their views about themselves, their jobs, and their boss have affected their performance on the job. A person like this has already decided that nothing will change in his career and that he has no power over his future. Viewing yourself this way is a sure way of keeping yourself from doing all you can do on your job, and more.

Whatever you do for a living do your best at it. Don't land the job that you have been working so hard to get, and then become lazy once you get it. Don't be afraid of the challenges that your new job will require of you. View these challenges as a chance to excel in the workplace. Work as though it's your last job.

"Whatever thy hand findeth to do, do it with thy might; for there is no work, nor device, nor knowledge, nor wisdom, in the grave, whither thou goest"

(Ecclesiastes 9:11).

Whether you are in a workplace, or any type of organization where there is more than one person working together toward a single goal, this book is for you. I invite you to read this book with an open heart and mind in order to make the necessary corrections in your life and apply the principles to your daily duties and responsibilities.

You may only have one chance to put forth your best effort while you are on this earth; do it with excellence in mind. It is for sure you will only get one life to live on this earth. Strive to use what God has given you to do your best at what you do.

Sincerely,
James Puckett

Foreword

This is one book every manager will want every team member to read. Powerful! To the point! Organizations are built around these principles and if embraced they are life changing.

You help me reset my commitment to excellence!

You make me want to continue to always do my best. Your book is inspiring. Great Job!

Hallerin Hilton Hill
Radio & Television Host

Foreword

Have you grown complacent in your job? Are you fighting feelings of dissatisfaction at your work place? If so, this book is for you. In James Puckett's new book, *When the Boss is Not Looking*, you will be renewed like eagles with valuable insight and biblical direction that is given page after page to redirect workplace negativity with God's hope.

As an educator, coming off of summer break is always a difficult time. It seems that you just get used to being off of work and then you are right back in the daily grind. I read *When the Boss is Not Looking* my first week back from summer break, and I felt the book was written especially for me! The scriptures references refreshed my spirit and reminded me of what God expects of me. The inspired words pierced my spirit and my heart. I plan on keeping the book close by so that I can reread passages for daily devotions and inspiration.

Dr. Jill Hobby
Assistant Principal
Northwest Middle School
Knoxville, Tennessee

Foreword

In response to the Pharisees' question as to a person's responsibility to civil government and worldly obligations, Jesus replied simply to "Render therefore unto Caesar the things which are Caesar's; and unto God the things that are God's" (Matthew 22:21). In this statement, Christ outlines our commitment to the things of this world, whether it is to our family, our country, or our job.

Christians have always had to live in two worlds at the same time. Our faith in Christ gives us the hope of an afterlife in His presence. However, we cannot lose sight of walking with Christ in the present physical world, giving to our own personal Caesars. Christ was quite direct in ideas on stewardship and personal accountability. In the Gospel of Luke, there are two parables that reflect on someone losing something of value, and being the good steward, taking the time and effort to fulfill their obligations and find, that which was in their charge. There is great rejoicing when the shepherd finds his lost sheep, as well as the woman who finds her missing piece of silver.

Through his birth, his death, and his resurrection, Christ fulfilled a covenant that delivered us to our salvation. We as Christians are in Christ's image, and inasmuch, need to fulfill the commitments and obligations that we make.

In this work, "When the Boss is Not Looking", James Puckett examines our responsibilities as Christians in the workplace in fulfilling our duty and obligations to our employer. In this work, Puckett examines how our attitude and motivations for working at a particular place reflect on our character and how we are viewed as a person. He also examines our relationship with our boss and our ethical obligations we have to our employer. He concludes the work with an examination of being consistent at work, and ensuring our actions are consistent with who we are as a person.

In being good and faithful stewards in our workplace and by honoring the commitments that we make with our employer in this life, we model the commitment that Christ fulfilled for us in His death, burial, and resurrection that gives us the promise of a life in Him after this life. This is our duty and responsibility as Christians.

Mark Roy
Kroger Manager
Knoxville, Tennessee

Foreword

God wants his best for all of us. Are you achieving your best? If you are only going through the motions at work, have no passion for what you are doing or not respecting your leaders then you are not fully using the gifts and talents God has given you on your job. James' book, When the Boss is Not Looking, gives practical advice on how to get promoted and further your success while maintaining integrity on your job. We all want to achieve a greater level of success, but being obedient to God and being in His perfect will for your life is the important thing. This is a relevant topic today as we live in a time where getting ahead at all cost is common practice. It is easy to justify your way into believing that it is okay to compromise work ethics on your job. In fact, you may have justified your behavior because you feel you are underpaid, or perhaps you think that your boss does not appreciate you and your efforts go unnoticed. However, God is always looking out for you and your best interests. The things that appear to go unnoticed, God notices. James challenges the reader to be a person of good character and examine his motives and attitudes towards his boss and the company. Are you acting in the best interest of your company? Examine the driving force behind your work habits. Do you have your boss's best interest at heart or is it your paycheck? Be a person of your word and demonstrate stability and consistency that your boss can rely on. By focusing your efforts on contributing to your company's success, in time you will reap benefits such as increased pay and position.

I have known James Puckett for many years. He is a faithful church member, educator for the challenged in the public school system, honorable retired military Chief Warrant

Officer and respected friend. This is his seventh book. In this book, James highlights 11 steps to help propel you toward success in the workplace, one of which is positive self-talk. Remind yourself what God says about you. He also talks about how hard it is to rise above education. Take the necessary steps to obtain the highest level of education possible. Accomplishment comes when you have vision. Write your vision down and keep it before you. These are all powerful truths that James illustrates in his book. He further explains how loyalty and willingness to serve your leaders prepares you for leadership one day. Jesus himself in Matthew 20:28 says, "Just as the Son of Man did not come to be served but to serve." That should be how we live our life in the workplace and beyond. <u>When the Boss is Not Looking</u> is an excellent book detailing the importance of being obedient to God; no matter what position you may have in the workplace. Everyone has a purpose and everyone has been given an assignment. Your purpose is significant. Your job in life does not define you; however, the way in which you perform your job when no one is looking speaks volumes about who you are. Don't wait until your ideal job comes along or you get the big promotion to make your life count. In order to receive God's best for your life remember the journey is as important as the destination. Start incorporating these principles today and begin to live your best life now.

Howard L. Sentell III
Tammy Sentell
Business Owners
Knoxville, Tennessee

Foreword

How do you act when no one is looking? This is what truly defines a person's character. This book takes it one step further – into the workplace. Author James Puckett asks how do you act <u>When the Boss is Not Looking</u>? He offers many thoughts and ideas that any employee, young or old, should contemplate, hopefully prior to accepting a job. We all would be wise to evaluate ourselves using James' book as a template, and do so on a regular basis. A person needs to assess:

- Do I have the character to do <u>this</u> job the best I can?
- Can I make a commitment to follow my boss's vision?
- Am I able to be loyal to my employer's wishes?
- Can I meet their expectation and do so consistently?

James will help you realize that it is necessary to do all of this if you truly want to be of value to your employer and in turn to yourself. Many employers will challenge their employees to evaluate themselves and their job, but sadly many employers don't. This is when you need to follow James' guide to self-evaluation.

As a young man I prayed to always be placed in positive environments. I particularly wanted to have a career environment that would give me the pride that made me want to give it my all. I wanted a career that I didn't care if the boss was *looking*, because I always gave my all. My prayers were answered when I became a Chick-fil-A owner/operator 25 years ago. With God's blessings I personally don't worry about any boss watching. My wish is that after reading <u>When the Boss is Not Looking</u> that you too will find the peace that comes with knowing you are where God wants you to be. This peace will help you commit to do your best and receive your just rewards.

Marshall Wilkins
Chick-fil-A Owner/Operator
Knoxville, Tennessee

Foreword

As an Education Director in a Beauty School I have been in the work place both as an employee and an employer. Understanding the importance of maintaining certain standards in the work area is vital to a successful work environment. The values that this book portrays are extremely necessary not only because it is biblically correct but also because it works. I know that it is Brother Puckett's intention to help anyone who is looking for direction, and I believe that following the principles found in his book will help to guide you into success.

Gabriela Gagnier
Educational Director
Knoxville Institute of Hair Design

Foreword

When James asked me to write a foreword to his book, *When the Boss Is Not Looking*, I was honored. As a business owner, I am truly concerned with the attitude, character, and ethics of the people I employ. I can't watch everything every employee does all of the time. However, just as employers will notice excellence, so too will they notice slothfulness and indifference. Equally importantly, I am the parent of two teenagers. It is my job to try to instill good work habits in them so that they may become productive members of society. I feel that subjects covered in this book are as important as any other subject being taught in our schools today. I wish every person would be encouraged to read *When The Boss Is Not Looking*.

Answering this honestly is the first step to being a better employee. Ask yourself this, "If you were the boss and knew what you know about yourself would you hire, retain, or promote you?" Everyone can strive to do a better job. Here is a question someone asked me and I like to ask young students. It helped me to know what I wanted in the way of a job. It goes like this: Let's say I gave you $100 million and told you that you could keep it; it is yours with one stipulation, you have to choose a job right now. You must work eight hours a day, five days a week, fifty weeks a year, for the next fifty years. You have to stick with it; no changing or you have to give all the money back. I believe if you take the money out of the equation most people will choose to do what is truly their passion. If you only work for money you may never be content. You can make less money and be doing something you like and find more joy in it.

Character plays a huge role in how well you do in life; not only your job. Someone once said, "Character is doing the right thing even if no one is watching." You will have choices on any job to prove if you have good or poor character. Who knows who is watching you? You may say, "I don't care, this is not what I am going to do forever." Remember when you apply for that new job you don't want that "don't care" attitude to be the only thing that your former boss remember about you.

If your boss puts trust in you, prove him right! He may be looking for any excuse to promote you or give you a raise. He apparently is looking for or has seen something in you to put the trust of his business in you. His family's income and his reputation rides on you. In fact, your income and your fellow employee's income may be riding on you doing your best - even when the boss is not looking.

J. Craig Smith
Owner
Drive Rite Driving School
Knoxville, Tennessee

Chapter One

Your Motive for Working

Someone or something motivated you to work where you work. It may have been a friend, a relative, or a former co-worker. It may have been the location of the employment, the pay and benefits, the employer's track record, the type of work, the work schedule, or the dress code. It could have been one of these or a combination of these or something else that impressed you. If we are honest, we all will admit that pay and benefits are most likely the two top motivators for working where we work.

Money seems to get everyone's attention. One of the first questions we all have is "How much does the job pay?" And the second is "What type of benefits does the job offer?" We pay our bills with money. We receive many services for the exchange of money. The Bible says, "...*but money answereth all things*" *(Ecclesiastes 10:19)*. I am not suggesting that money should not be a motivator for working at a certain job. But if money is the main factor for working, it will bring out all the bad character flaws in you. You have to learn to love what you do without money, benefits, or anything else moving you. Your service on your job is important. If it were not, you probably wouldn't have been hired to fill the position. We must be careful that we don't let our motives for things get in the way of us providing the service that we were hired to provide. If money becomes the motive and not the service, we start to feel as though we are just there to fill a position.

After you have landed the job, your motive should change. If money or something else was your motive for working where you work, once you begin work, you should now strive to be the best employee that you can be. Your excitement turns from the money and benefits to providing a service. There should be a power now moving within you to help make your workplace safer, more enjoyable, and more productive all because you care about what you do and honor whom you do it for. *"And whatsoever ye do, do it heartily, as to the Lord, and not unto men" (Colossians 3:23).* First, you must realize that God made it possible for you to get the job. Secondly, your employer has given you the opportunity to work. If you are working to receive a paycheck you've missed the whole reason for doing what you do. Even if promotion is not looking too promising at the time, your motive should be to provide the service that you were hired to provide. Even if you and your boss don't always see eye-to-eye, you were not hired to get along with your boss, so keep your eyes on your job and do what you were hired to do. You should be thankful that you have a job and are able to go to it every day. This alone should be motivation enough for you to work hard even when the boss is not looking. Get excited about your job and the service you provide, and you will be motivated to a whole new level. Remember your co-workers are watching you. Give them an example to follow.

Know the Vision and Mission for What You Do

I believe that it's important to know the bigger picture of your job. What is the vision and mission of your company? What are the short and long term goals in your area of responsibility? What is your role and what are your responsibilities in helping obtain the vision and goals of your company? Your goal should be to share these goals with your boss and your coworkers. I think it is somewhat frustrating to perform a duty and not have a vision of what the outcome is to be. And I suggest that it would be a good thing to know the vision prior to taking on the task at hand.

"And the Lord answered me, and said, write the vision, and make it plain upon tables, that he may run that readeth it"

(Habakkuk 2:2).

If you know the vision of your employer and your boss, you can work with the joy of mind that you are a necessary team worker who is helping place the pieces on the puzzle even when the boss is not looking. You should work to take on the vision of your employer and boss. The mission of your job should be to make your boss's job as easy as possible. If your boss's daily workload is more than yours is, you need to catch the vision and put your hands to more of the work. Your vision should be to learn all you can about your job so that you can provide your boss with insight and ideas about how to make things better. As you help others in pursuit of their vision you might just discover your mission on earth.

Your Attitude While Working

Someone once said, "Your attitude determines your altitude." Your attitude at work will determine your level of performance on the job. Your attitude will affect your character. Or, you could reverse it and say that your character determines your attitude. I do not mean to insult anyone but your character says a lot about you as a person. Your character really defines who you are from the inside out. You may say, "I don't have very good character qualities." I believe that all character qualities can be improved upon. If you have a poor attitude about your job I believe that you can change your way of thinking. I find myself doing a lot of "self-talk" on my job, especially if something upsets me or operations just aren't going according to plan. Where I worked for seven, almost always things didn't go the way I had planned. Whatever my flesh was telling me to do or say I just did the opposite. Just because I felt a certain way, or people around me was doing or saying certain things, I could never loose focus that I had a job to do. My boss and co-workers were counting on me to perform. I had made a conscious decision to never let myself be cast down *(Psalm 42:5)*.

You should always perform on your job as if the boss was always looking. You should do your job as though there is a micro-camera watching you at all times. If you are a lazy person your character will show it on your job. If you are a hard working person who does what he is hired to do, your character will also show it on your job. Your character will not let you hide who you really are as a person. You may try to cover it up and may be successful at it for some time, but the truth of who you really are will be revealed through your character. All this starts with your attitude. Maybe the reason you haven't been promoted on your job is because you possess a negative attitude about what you do or the person you work for. Work like your boss is always watching. Your character will always produce the type of attitude you have on your job even if the boss is looking.

An attitude of gratitude on the job will take you much farther than an attitude of complaining. For seven years I worked at a local high school attending to children who have special needs. I went to work every day not knowing what the day was going to bring. Yes, I used my faith and expected to have a day without any major crises, but I couldn't control other people actions. But what I could control was how I reacted to any negative action. I had to make a conscious decision to prepare myself for what could happen on the job that day. It was important that I had the right attitude when I walked inside the building and was ready and willing to do whatever my boss needed done, or ready to confront any given situation. I had to be ready to adjust at a moment's notice. I believe that every person has the ability or can learn to choose his or her day on the job. I know that certain things are out of our control, but if we are in control of our emotions and feelings we can decide what type of day we have on the job. But I believe that many people let others' action or challenges on their job dictate what their performance will be like on that day. That's why the Bible tells us to guard our heart. Because it is out of our heart that we can determine how we act and react to certain situations *(Proverbs 4:23)*. I have worked with some people that complain about something from the time they walk in the door in the morning until they walk out the door in the afternoon. And many of these things could be changed if they chose to take control of the situation. Instead of making the necessary changes to make life on their job better they would rather complain all day.

Always strive to do more than you are required to do. People who only do the minimum requirements will most likely goof-off when the boss is not looking. My boss was good by herself, but my job was to make her great. Having this type of attitude on your job will help you perform to your maximum capacity even when the boss is not looking.

Some people are difficult to work for. But we should try to maintain a positive attitude so that we can get along with our boss. I can say without reservation that I was blessed those seven years where I worked. My boss was incredible at her job. She holds an extraordinary talent at what she does. The first day she walked in the classroom I knew she was good and part of my job was to make her better. I hope I have done this in some way. When the news came that she was moving out of the city it broke my heart. I did not want to see her go. I felt that we had a strong working relationship that could stand up against anything. I miss her, but I am comforted that I did my best to make her first job as a special education teacher a success. I hope that wherever she goes and whatever she does she will reflect on my attitude while she was my boss. I hope that she will be able to gain strength from the memories of our workplace. You should be so tuned-in with your boss that your whole focus on your job is to make him great at what he does. This type of relationship will not come without the right attitude while doing what you do, and whom you do it for.

Keep Your Work and Personal Life Separate

Whatever might have happened between the wife, the husband, the children, the dog, or maybe someone cut you off in traffic on your way to work, all these things must not be allowed to enter into your work place. Your workplace is not a place to bring all your personal problems. If you get in the habit of bringing your problems to work, you will lose focus on your primary task. Others will think it is alright to bring and discuss their personal problems into the work place. Remember your primary responsibility is to provide a service or produce a product.

Everyone has personal problems. You must learn to deal with your personal problems on personal time. When you are on the job that time belongs to your boss and employer even if they are not looking. If we are honest we all will admit to using employer's time to take care of personal issues. I am guilty of this myself. But one thing I practice is to not let outside issues and problems interfere with my job. Each morning when I walked through those doors I become a different person, - Not my personality, but my focus. My boss needed me to be 100% focused, alert, attentive, and active. I was ready to perform whatever task may arise.

There may be times when you might feel it is important to inform or discuss personal problems with your supervisor or a trusted co-worker. Try to do this during break times or over lunch if the environment warrants this. It may be more appropriate to ask your supervisor or a co-worker if you could speak with them a few minutes after work. However you choose to share your personal problems with others do it respectfully and professionally. You may work in a place where you can talk openly while attending to assigned work. But do not let this become a habit and have respect for those around you, because they may be easily distracted by your conversation.

Do not misunderstand me; I know that not talking about your problems will not make them go away. But it will be hard for you to talk about your problems without acting out your feelings. Talking about your problems won't make you feel any better. But it could make you sick. We are told to magnify the Lord and exalt His name, not our problems *(Psalm 34:3)*. We should strive to be more of a person of gratitude. Bringing all your personal problems on your job is not only a hindrance to you but to your co-workers also. When you bring your personal problems to work with you there is a decrease in your ability to function and keep your mind on the things you were assigned to do. When this happens your co-workers or others will be challenged to step in and pick up the slack. This could cause tension in the work place, which could slow down production or create poor quality of service. If you work at a job that requires your constant attention like I do, you should make every effort to make yourself and your service available when needed. And I feel that you should do this with a smile. Sometimes just putting a smile on your face can change your whole attitude for the better. Not to say what it might do for someone else who might be having a rough day.

"A merry heart doeth good like a medicine: but a broken spirit drieth the bones" (Proverbs 17:22). Keeping a merry heart on your job will help you better perform your daily duties. A merry heart will cause you to take the focus off your problems and look at the needs of others.

Your boss or employer may allow you to do things on the job that is personal in nature to you. Be respectful of the time and do not abuse it. Remember it is the boss's time and he needs you and your service, and is counting on your involvement in the work place. Sometimes we tend to get overwhelmed with our problems and we lose focus of what we are really supposed to be doing on the job. We are a self-serving people, and can sometimes forget about the mission and vision of the boss or employer. And above all, remember you are there to provide a service even when the boss is not looking.

Personal Journal Page

Chapter Two

Work Hard at What You Do

"Far and away the best prize that life has to offer is the chance to work hard at work worth doing."

- Theodore Roosevelt

If you believe that the work you are doing is worth doing, then you should work hard at it. I do not want to mislead anyone into thinking that their value in life is solely found in what they do. We all know that achieving goals in life makes us feel a sense of self-worth about ourselves. We must understand that our real value in life does not come from what we do, but comes from who we are. But what you do and how you do it is important. In my previous book, *24/7 Success: Living a Lifetime of Success,* I pointed out the important of working hard. Every person who works a job must be willing to work hard at it even when the boss is not looking.

Every person has the potential to work hard but it is a choice that he makes. When God created man He just didn't create him so that He would have someone to share fellowship with, or use up the gifts of the earth, but man was also created to work on this earth.

"And God created man in His own image, in the image of God created he him; male and female created He them. And God blessed them, and God said unto them, Be fruitful, and multiply, and replenish the earth, and subdue it: and have

dominion over the fish of the sea, and over the fowl of the air, and over every living thing that moveth upon the earth"

(Genesis 1:27-28).

God gave the command, but it will not automatically happen. What God has created man to do will now require hard work on his part. Being fruitful, multiplying, replenishing, and subduing the earth we live on will take some hard work. You shouldn't even think about success until you can hold down a steady job and are willing to commit to working hard at it. You will never experience any level of success in life if you are unwilling to work hard whether the boss is looking or not. God is serious about man working and pulling his load. The Bible states if a man won't work, he should not be allowed to eat *(2 Thessalonians 3:10).* We should learn a lesson from the ant *(Proverbs 6:6-11).* The Bible teaches that the ant is diligent in its business in life. The ant is busy in gathering food for the winter, and saving for the future. The ant is not lazy, but a hard worker. The ant does not care if someone is watching him or not. He is diligent about his business - hard working. The ant knows that no other insect is going to do it for him. No one is going to do it for you.

In today's society and culture many people do not take hard work serious. They go about on their jobs with the attitude that someone else will do it. Most people do not know what hard physical work is. But I believe in order for you to experience any level of success in life, a period of hard work is necessary especially when the boss is not looking. If you teach yourself to work hard when the boss is not looking, then when the boss is looking you won't have to fake it. Having this type of attitude on your first job will make it easier as you advance in the workforce.

Whatever you find your hands to do, do it with all your heart. What did your boss see in you the day he interviewed you? What was his first impression of you on your first day at work? Someone once said, "It only takes seven seconds to form an opinion of another person and during those seven seconds eleven impressions are formed." You may be saying, "I do not care what my boss thinks of me!" The impressions that your boss have of you could be the link between you losing or keeping your job. If you want to make a different where you work learn to work hard at what you do. Your boss shouldn't have to tell you more than one time that something needs to be done. If you are really concerned and have a zeal for your work, you have properly already figured out what it is that needs to be done. But your boss does not want to tell you more than once to take care of something at work. He does not have time to constantly check behind you to see if you are doing your job. When you take the attitude of working hard you are also taking an attitude of doing what you were hired to do without the boss telling you, or when he is not looking.

"Act as if what you do makes a difference. It does."

- William James
American Psychologist and Philosopher

Obeying Leadership While Working

Someone once said, "I don't have a problem with authority, I just have a problem with someone telling me what to do." People who think and feel this way not only have a problem with someone telling them what to do, but they also have a problem with life. Most of our lives are lived with someone telling us what to do and what not to do. Authority has been around since the beginning of man and will be around even after you are gone. All throughout the Bible we read how God wants to be the leader of our lives. In the society we live in there is a form of leadership everywhere we look. There is leadership in the church, in the schools, in the market places, in the prisons, in the home, and on your job. Whoever your leader happens to be, remember you didn't put him there and chances are you won't succeed in removing him. If there is leadership you just can't deal with on your job, then it may be time for you to find other employment. But don't be surprised that when you get to your next job, there will be someone there telling you what to do.

There will always be someone higher up the chain than you. Your boss has a boss. Your boss's boss has a boss. Their leadership may not be close by, but they are expected to obey it even if it is a thousand miles away. I can tell you a thing or two about obeying leadership. I spent nearly twenty-five years in the military and during that time not one day went by without someone giving me orders to do something. Oh yes, I gave orders too, but I also had to obey the orders and commands that were issued to me. It goes both ways. I believe that every good leader at sometime was an obedient servant. I believe that before anyone can become a good leader, they must prove to be a good follower, even when the boss is not looking.

I think some people are under the impression that they have to like their boss before it is required for them to do their job. I will be the first to tell you that it would help if you and your boss did get along well on the job. But even if you cannot stand your superior, you are committed to your employer. Your boss did not force you to take the job. I believe that many times people curse the very resources that God put in their lives. Be thankful for your job, your employer, your co-workers, and your boss. It may not be the place that you plan to stay for the rest of your life, but that is where you are right now. If you cannot find something good about your boss and your job then you need to seriously think about going elsewhere. The Bible says, "to obey is better than sacrifice..." *(1 Samuel 15:22).* Obeying leadership on your job will take you a long way in life.

Loyalty to your boss is a character that has been lost in the workplace of today. You should have a certain level of respect for your boss. This doesn't mean that you are required to hang out with your boss on the weekend or visit his home regularly. But there should be a working bond between you and him in the workplace. You should support his plans and do all you can to help see them come to pass. You should never do anything on your job to disgrace your boss or the company. I am not suggesting that you be a doormat and ignore issues that may arise. Part of being a loyal employee is speaking up and talking to your boss when you do not agree with something. You are entitled to your opinion, but you are not entitled to always get your way. There will be times when you will voice your concerns but nothing will change. You are still required to be loyal to your boss even when he is not looking. Because you committed yourself when you were hired, you are required to defend your boss. Your boss may not have the perfection you think he should have, but you are still required to be totally loyal to your boss and carry out your duties at work. I am not suggesting that you be loyal to illegal, immoral, and unethical things. But just being offensive and non-compliant about everything your boss does is not loyalty. It is not easy being loyal when you know you are being taken advantage of. It is not easy being loyal when you know you are being used. It is not easy being loyal when you feel like quitting and walking. But I have learned that loyalty is not a feeling but an act. Just remember you may be in a leadership position some day, and you will depend upon the loyalty of your employees when times are hard. Most of the times these are just tests that we are required to pass in order to move through the valley that we find ourselves in. Continue being faithful and loyal and you will slowly see your way out. There is a moral and ethical escape for every temptation.

Personal Journal Page

Chapter Three

You Are Only as Good as Your Word

"When thou vowest a vow unto God, defer not to pay it; for he hath no pleasure in fools: pay that which thou hast vowed. Better is it that thou shouldest not vow, than that thou shouldest vow and not pay"
(Ecclesiastes 5:4-5).

Your word is your bond between you and your boss. As much as it lies within us, we should keep our word to our employers. When we do not live up to our word we lose all credibility with those who are counting on us. We will either have good credit or bad credit with our boss. I believe that there are two things that will determine your reputation on your job – your work ethics, and keeping your word. When you were hired for the job, your employer found you creditable just as you trusted them. You were hired on the belief that you were capable and willing to do the job, and you accepted the job with the belief that you would be paid for the work you did. One of the credentials you presented was your word. When we fail to do what we were hired to do our employer now has to take disciplinary action and possibly hire someone else for the job. At this point your "word" becomes discredited with your boss and your employer. Just as a physician wants high creditability with his patients, a boss and employer wants high creditability with his workers and employees. *"But whoso keepeth his word, in him verily is the love of God perfected: hereby know we that we are in him" (1 John 2:5).*

Whether or not you keep your word will depend on the state of your integrity. Integrity deals with the whole moral character of a man. As I mentioned in chapter one your character defines you as a person. Your character determines how you act from day to day. I believe that character is taught and not learned. Somewhere during your lifetime you were taught by someone or something to do the things you do and act the way you act. Our habits in life are a result of our character. Every time we choose to do something, or act a certain way, we are revealing our character. Therefore, you can teach yourself to keep your word. Maybe you haven't had anyone model this but you can teach yourself. Every bad habit or good habit springs out of our character. It comes from the core of our heart. Character says, "I have integrity." Integrity says, "I am honest and can be trusted."

Imagine promising your child day after day that you are going to attend one of his baseball games. Every time a game is scheduled your schedule at work changes and you cannot make the game. The child comes to you again and again telling you about a game that is coming up, you make a promise to be there but on game day something comes up and you can't be there. Your child may or may not understand your reasons for you not being there but he now feels that he cannot trust you at your word. Your creditability with your child as it relates to what you tell him is now damaged. When you said "yes", you signed a verbal covenant with him and you did not keep your part of the deal.

Husbands and wives give their word to each other in marriage vows. Parents give their word to their children when they are born. A church congregation gives their word to the pastor. Christians give their word to God when they are saved. Employees give their word to their employers when they are hired. I think most of the time people go back on their word because it becomes an inconvenience for them to keep it. Sometimes keeping our word will inconvenience us but if you are to be a person of integrity you must keep your word at all costs.

I recall when I was ministering at a local nursing home on Sunday mornings before I went to church. It was not always easy for me to get there. During that time I was still on active military duty. Some Sundays I had military obligations but I still kept my word and went. I gave my word to the coordinator that I would be there every Sunday morning at a certain time to conduct ministry if I were in town. My military duties sometimes required me to travel. I honored my word until my military obligations required me to move out of the city. The Bible is clear on making sure we can follow through on the commitments we make *(Luke 14:28-35)*. I could have gone when I felt like it or when it was convenient for me, but my name was on the line. My reputation as a person was being challenged. Every time we commit to do something we put our character and integrity on display. I believe the quickest way to damage a relationship is to go back on your word. There will be times when your boss will change. But it should not change you or your work ethics.

When we give our word, our honesty and trustworthiness is at stake. Your name is now at stake. *"A good name is better than precious ointment....."(Ecclesiastes 7:1)*. If you do have to leave your present employer and take on another job, it would be best for you to leave there with a good report that you can take to your next job. I am not talking about being perfect in our human nature, because no one is perfect. But the goal is to give our word with the full intention that we will keep it even if the boss is not looking. *"And whatever ye do in word or deed, do all in the name of the Lord Jesus, giving thanks to God and the Father by Him"* *(Colossians 3:17)*. Everyone who has a job should go to work every day, be on time, and give their boss an honest day's work for an honest day's pay even when he is not looking.

I believe it is disrespectful to your boss and co-workers for you to continue to show-up late to your job day after day. I wonder how quickly we could correct ourselves if our employer informed us that we had to start clocking in and out every day and we would be only paid for the time we worked? Most of us would probably straighten up pretty fast. No one is going to wait on you or I to show up at our jobs for work to be done. If we can get to other places on time, i.e. hair appointments, doctor appointments, social functions appointments, then we should without hesitation get to work on time even when the boss is not looking.

Personal Journal Page

Chapter Four

When You Feel Your Pay Doesn't Equal Your Labor

If I were a betting man, I would bet that every person who now works or has worked in the past has felt or thought that he was not being paid enough for the work he does. Sometimes we all may feel this way. There will be circumstances where you work or serve that will cause you to feel and talk this way. If you were to take a survey asking people if they feel that their pay equals their work, a majority of the answers would be "no". But there are those people whose work does not equal what they are paid. To put it another way would be to say, "they are not doing the amount of work that they are paid to do." Maybe you are only being paid the minimum wage, but this is no reason to do any less work than you were hired to do. After all you did ask for the job and after you sign on the dotted line, you have committed to that employer or company that you will give them a decent day's work for an honest day's pay. Some people get up every morning and go to their job with the mindset of doing the bare minimum. These people will never see past the dollar signs. More pay will always be on their mind. They will find and make excuses to become slothful in their work, especially when the boss is not looking. *"My little children, let us not love in word, neither in tongue; but in deed and in truth" (1John 3:18).* Whatever negative feelings you may have about your boss or job, get past them and start doing the job you were hired to do even if the boss is not looking. If your sole reason for going to your job is to earn a paycheck, you have the wrong mindset.

If you put the money before your responsibilities and duties you will miss a great opportunity to prove your self-worth. Every chance I get to talk to young people on this subject I always say to them, "If you desire to own your own business, don't do it to make money, but do it to provide a service. If you are good at what you do the money will come." I have come to understand that the money is a bi-product of the quality of service rendered. Too many times we focus on the dollars and overlook the quality of service we are providing to the people. Many employees do the same thing where they work. They focus on what they are being paid rather than focus on their quality of work.

When Your Work Becomes Slothful

"The achievements of an organization are the results of the combined effort of each individual."

- Vince Lombardi

Constantly dwelling on and talking about how you are not being adequately paid on your job will make you sluggish in your performance on the job. Sluggishness will make you habitually lazy. Employers don't want slothful people working for them. When they hired you, they hired you to do a job. They entrusted you with stewardship over a portion of the company. They put trust in you that you will be diligent in your work and that you will complete your assigned tasks. People who do not understand stewardship or do not care about another's affairs will become slothful in their daily duties on the job. You will gradually start to drop off in your performance. Eventually laziness will set in and the only time you make an attempt to fulfill your assigned duties will be when you know the boss is looking. If you are a poor steward of that which you have been entrusted with, you are taking something that doesn't belong to you or you didn't earn. This is stealing. Your job has rules and guidelines that you are obligated to follow. Your boss or employer expects you to report to work at a certain time, perform certain tasks, follow certain rules, and conduct yourself in a certain manner. If we focus too much on anything outside of our job we will become poor stewards over our jobs. When this happens we neglect our responsibilities and leave them to someone else to take care of. We pretend to perform our duties only until the boss is not looking. Do your job well and try to be the best at what you do. Your boss will recognize and appreciate your service.

I wonder how much money is lost in production each year because of slothfulness. When slothfulness is present in a person, wastefulness becomes visible. A person can waste many man-hours on the job. He gets to work late. He stands around and does nothing. He takes unauthorized long breaks. He goes to lunch early and returns late. Sometimes he even leaves for the day early. But he expects to get paid what the employer promised. Well, why not give your employer what he expects of you and what you have promised him even if he is not looking.

"He also that is slothful in his work is brother to him that is a great waster"
(Proverbs 18:9).

I try to live with the thought in mind that someone who went before me contributed to the foundation of life that I am now enjoying and building upon. Whatever type of job we are working at someone worked hard to make that company what it is today. You or I have no right to try and tear it down by working slothfully and not doing our job. I think it would take less effort to destroy a business than it would to maintain it. What you do and how you do it, matters. Why do you think family businesses are so successful? Every member of the family involved understands that the success of the business depends on the discipline and hard work of each individual. And because every member sows into the business they have the right to eat from it, present and future profits. Every link in the chain has to hold its load. Every link in the chain knows that the other links are supported by it. If there is any weak link in the chain, over time, the business will fail. It is the same on your job. When someone on your job is not pulling his or her load, the whole organization suffers. When every person does his or her part all is rewarded. When we build upon the things that the company or business was founded on, we will enjoy the rewards of the past, present and future.

"According to the grace of God which is given unto me, as a wise masterbuilder, I have laid the foundation, and another buildeth thereon. But let every man take heed how he buildeth thereupon"
(1 Corinthians 3:10).

When you were hired, you were hired for the good of the company or business. Think about it. What company or business would hire you if they thought you were going to destroy their business? You were hired based on your qualifications and skills and the belief that you would be an asset to the business and not a debt. You were hired to be one of the team players. I believe most people who do not enjoy their job have not invested their best in it. When you invest yourself in your job, you will respect it and treat it with pride.

I remember working part-time at a retail auto parts store some years ago. I was being paid by the hour. A large portion of my responsibility was working the cash register. When business was slow there were lots of other things in the store that needed attending to. One day business had slowed down and I went on the floor to straighten the items on the shelves, as I usually did when I had no customers to wait on. One of my co-worker said to me, "James, why don't you sit down, you are making me look bad." He was offended by the fact that I was keeping myself busy while he was standing around talking while on the clock. It was quite obvious that my co-worker had developed this attitude and habits early in his life. I believe that the habits we practice in our former days, if not corrected, we will carry over into our latter days. If you are slothful and lazy on your first job, you will take those same attitudes and behaviors to you next job. They will follow you every where you go.

If you really respect your employer or boss, and appreciate what he does for you, then show him. Try getting to work five or ten minutes earlier once in a while. Do a little more than you are asked to do. Your boss will love you for it and you will feel better about yourself and your ability to perform on your job. And get ready for the rewards and favor because they are coming. Believe me, people do notice a job well done.

Personal Journal Page

Chapter Five

Be a Person of Consistency Where You Work

How consistent are you on your job? Do you go to work every day? Do you arrive to work on time every day? Do you always return back to work on time after your breaks? Do you always try to do your very best each day? Are you always honest and true with your boss? Are you honest and true to yourself? Are you prompt in doing the things you are asked to do? What did your boss see in you the day he interviewed you? Does he see the same qualities today? What was his first impression of you on your first day at work? Does he have the same impression about you today? These are just a few questions we should ask ourselves to determine how consistent we are on our job. Consistency prepares you for that next promotion. Consistency says, "I am a leader in the making." Leaders are self-made. Leaders will recognize there is a need and then find ways to meet or fulfill that need. Your boss can't create or make a leader out of you unless you are willing to lead. Your boss can give you the opportunity to lead but you must do the work and the things to show him that you are ready for that position. Consistency is one of those things. When you are inconsistent on your job you are saying to your boss "I am not ready for the next step up. I am not ready for promotion." Coming to work on time two or three days out of the week and being late the other days is a sure sign that you are not ready for a leadership position. Being a person of consistency is not only important on your job, but also in your home, and where you worship. Consistency is important because it shows others that you care and you are there to serve them. Consistency proves that you are reliable and accountable. Consistency is a test to determine if you are worthy of more responsibility. There is nothing worse than having a co-worker who is unreliable and unaccountable.

I am reminded of how hard my parents worked to make a living. My parents worked on a farm until I was about 11 or 12 years old. My dad and mom were sharecroppers during the fifties until the mid sixties. They worked consistently each week to keep the lights on and to buy food for a family of seven. If there wasn't much profit from the crops during the year, then the boss didn't do much sharing at the end of the year. My dad's amount would depend on the amount of profit gained that year. If it was a good crop year, the profits were good, at lest we thought so, but he only got a small percentage of that.

My parents were not well educated. They didn't graduate from high school. But Mom and Dad worked hard at what they did. They were in the fields day after day. They kept food on the table, clothes on our backs, shoes on our feet, and a roof over our heads. It took hard work on the part of the whole family. My parents taught me about staying at the things that were important in life. They taught me the important of being consistent. They taught me the important of being prompt in my duties and responsibilities.

It doesn't matter if you are working in a public or private place; your goal should be to work consistently at your job. Your boss where you work is counting on you to report to work everyday and be ready to do what you were hired to do. Your co-workers are counting on you to support, to help, to encourage, and to lead even when no one is looking.

Be a Person of Stability Where You Work

A person of stability is not quickly moved by uncertainty of events. One thing you must learn after you enter the work force is to be stable on your job. No employer likes an employee who is shaken by every change in policy. Life itself is a series of changes. Do not jump up and walk away from your job just because there was a change in the way the boss wants things done. Remember you gave your word and your name is on the line. Do not be a person who hops from job to job. I know there are times when a change in employment is necessary. But going from job to job just because you do not like what's taking place at your place of employment are signs that you are not stable. Stability means that you are planted. It means that you are fixed in what you do. You are fixed in mind, soul, and spirit. You are not easily overthrown by change on your job. You have established that place where you work as your place of duty. Stability is a character trait that will be tested from time to time. Show your boss that you have the strength to stand even in the worst of times on the job. In hard times your boss wants to know that he can count on you to dig both feet in and help get the job done.

Starting a new job is like putting a seed into the ground. If you dig up that seed before it has the chance to take root and spring up, that seed is no longer good for anything. You have destroyed everything that seed had the potential to produce. Where you work is the ground and you are the seed. Every time you leave one job and go to another, you have dug up your seed. It takes a seed a full season to develop a root system. Once that seed sprang forth out of the ground it has developed a root system, which is imperative for growth and productivity. When we take on a job, we are planting a seed in the company or business, and into our future. How long you stay at your job will determine how stable you are. Again, I know there are times and circumstances when a move is warranted. But just leaving because you don't like your boss or the way he does things, or changes were made and now you are required to move out of your comfort zone, is no real reason for leaving. To be stable at anything in life requires selflessness and commitment to a cause. Are you committed to your work?

The "Don't Care" Employee

It was hard for me to come to grips with myself to write this section. But after talking to God daily about these issues, I soon knew that God was speaking to me and saying, "Go Forth." So, here you have it.

I know that some people won't agree with me and will take issue with what I am about to say. I can only speak from my own personal experiences of working over the past thirty or forty years. Sometimes I wonder if it is just me that thinks and feels this way. Perhaps I am just a bit aggressive in approaching my work responsibilities, but I do not think it is a bad or evil thing. With that said, I do not apologize for what I am going to write here.

It just seems to amaze me how lazy, irresponsible, and disrespectful some people can be. Some people think that they can just show up late at their jobs and then do little or nothing. I have learned that some people just don't seem to get the idea of working to earn a living. The more you talk to them, it seems, the worse they get. I have just come to the conclusion that this type of employee simply doesn't care. They do not care about the counsel of their co-workers or the advice of their supervisors. They do not care what anyone says or thinks about their work performance.

I ask myself several times a day, "Why don't people do their share of the work in the workplace?" I am not talking about someone who is untrained or has not been instructed what to do and when to do it. I am talking about seasoned employees who have been on the job for a while, or at least long enough to know what to do. Well, every time I would ask myself why they are so lazy, irresponsible, and disrespectable, I always come up with the answer - they do not care.

I think it is irresponsible of any employee to sit back and watch their co-workers do all the work. I think it is just laziness on their part. It shows disrespect to the boss for an employee to sit back and watch him do the job that he hired someone to do, and the employee won't even offer a helping hand. And to make things worse, some people pick and chose what they feel comfortable doing or only do the things that won't get their hands dirty. I was not raised like this. Maybe this is the problem – not everyone has been taught to work hard and be responsible. I will accept that. But what excuse can be used after one has been instructed and shown what to do? What excuse can be used after being given one-on-one, hands on training? I have come to understand that these people do not care. Now it is time for some subordinate to subordinate counseling.

I spent almost twenty-five years in the military. I knew what it meant when one of my fellow soldiers gave me a little "correction talk." I knew that either I wasn't doing something that I should have been doing, or I was doing something that I should not have been doing. I knew that if I didn't want a superior soldier talking to me I had best take the advice of my subordinate. I know without a doubt that this played a major role in the success of my military career, and over time, my civilian career. Without the counsel of many subordinate soldiers my military career would have been cut short. Now I know that I am comparing a military job to a civilian job, but the principles work in the same way. Now I have to admit that some soldiers who got a talk from their subordinates didn't always take it to heart. It was not long before their superior was counseling them. Some received the counsel and got their act together while others shortened their time in military uniform. I learned in the military that it was always better to be counseled by someone who was on the same level as you than to be counseled by your boss.

Now after your subordinate has warned you and there is no change in your performance, what's next? After your boss has counseled you on your performance and there is no change, what's next? If you care anything about your job, receive the counsel of the subordinate. Correct your negative actions and get on the right track. But, if you don't receive the counsel of either it can only be said that you don't care.

So it doesn't matter whether the boss is looking or not, you just don't care. You will find over time that you are unable to hold any job for a long period of time due to your nonchalant attitude in the workplace. Do not let this happen to you.

Personal Journal Page

Chapter Six

The Boss is "Looking"

Your performance on the job is being evaluated every day you are there. Your boss has the responsibility and the right to edit your work. Some people may think this is micromanaging. But the truth of the matter is that it is his job. Who else is going to correct you when you are not performing to standard? Who else is qualified to monitor and evaluate your daily work? Yes, we should be doing this daily to ourselves, but how many of us will attempt to do this if we are not pulling our share of the workload? Every employee honestly should look at his quality of work on his job. He should evaluate himself to make sure he is doing at least what his duty description states or whatever your boss said you are responsible for doing, if not more.

Your boss where you work may not be able to keep a constant watch on you, but you are being watched. Your boss doesn't want to look at your performance every day and probably doesn't have the time to do this. Your boss wants to believe that every employee has put out 100% of their effort to pull their share of the workload. He does not want to think for one minute that someone on his team is doing less than his or her job calls for. Your boss is no fool. He knows when someone is not doing what he should be doing, or when an employee is not pulling his share of the load. This will be revealed by one of two ways. First, he will be seen constantly finding ways to get out of work. Secondly, it can cause strife in the workplace by stress shown in co-workers. Your boss knows more of what goes on in the workplace than you think, even when they are not looking directly at you.

But, you should not only be concerned about your boss at work, but about your Boss in heaven. Your heavenly Boss is looking at every move you make and He hears every non-working, inoperative, unemployed word that comes out of your mouth, on and off your job. You may be saying, "I am self-employed." Well, that's good. In chapter one, we discussed how our attitude determines how far we go on our job and in life. From that perspective we are all self-employed. Each person controls their success where they work. But if you are the sole proprietor of a business you should thank God that He has allowed you the opportunity to enjoy such privilege. But in the eyes of God there is no such thing as "Self-employed." You might be the sole owner of the business and make all the decisions. Really, God is the owner and you are the co-owner. He just gives you the responsibility of operating it. God also expect for you to be a faithful steward of all the things that He has placed in your control. This includes the resources, people, money, and time. All decisions you make you should consult with the owner first, because He is looking.

"The Lord is in his holy temple, the Lord's throne is in heaven: his eyes behold, his eyelids try, the children of men"

(Psalm 11:4).

"The eyes of the Lord are in every place, beholding the evil and the good"

(Proverbs 15:3).

"But I say unto you, That every idle word that men shall speak, they shall give account thereof in the day of judgment"

(Matthew 12:36).

So as you can see there is nothing you or I can get away with. We are being monitored and watched 24/7 by our heavenly Boss - God. If you are living for Him then you should want to please Him. One way you please Him is by doing what's right in His eyes - whatever you find your hands to do, do it unto Him and not man.

"Whatsoever thy hand findeth to do, do it with thy might; for there is no work, nor device, nor knowledge, nor wisdom, in the grave, whither thou goest"

(Ecclesiastes 9:10).

Personal Journal Page

Conclusion

I hope after reading this book you have started to look at your job and where you work with a different set of eyes. Start seeing your workplace and the company you work for as a special place and an elite group of people. When you are called to be part of an elite group, things will get harder not easier. But if you allow the challenges and trails to invade your world where you work, and you work through them not giving up, over time you will learn how to better deal with stress, challenges, and setbacks that life brings.

Read this book whenever you feel that you are not giving all you have to your job. Share this book with others who you know will benefit from it. Life is not easy, but you can enjoy the journey.

Scriptures Used in the Preparation of this Manuscript

And Samuel said, Hath the Lord as great delight in burnt offerings and sacrifices, as in obeying the voice of the Lord? Behold, to obey is better than sacrifice, and to hearken than the fat of rams. (1 Samuel 15:22)

The Lord is in His holy temple, the Lord's throne is in heaven; His eyes behold, His eyelids try, the children of men. (Psalm 11:4)

O magnify the Lord with me, and let us exalt His name together. (Psalm 34:3)

Why art thou cast down, O my soul? And why art thou disquieted in me? Hope thou in God: for I shall yet praise him for the help of His countenance. (Psalm 42:5)

Keep thy heart with all diligence: for out of it are the issues of life (Proverbs. 4:23)

The eyes of the Lord are in every place, beholding the evil and the good. (Proverbs 15:3)

A merry heart doeth good like a medicine: but a broken spirit drieth the bones. (Proverbs 17:22)

He also that is slothful in his work is brother to him that is a great waster. (Proverbs 18:9).

When thou vowest a vow unto God, defer not to pay it; for he hath no pleasure in fools: pay that which thou hast vowed. (Ecclesiastes 5:4)

Better is it that thou shouldest not vow, than that thou shouldest vow and not pay. (Ecclesiastes 5:5)

A good name is better than precious ointment; and the day of death than the day of one's birth. (Ecclesiastes 7:1)

Whatsoever thy hand findeth to do, do it with thy might; for there is no work, nor device, nor knowledge, nor wisdom, in the grave, whither thou goest. (Ecclesiastes 9:10)

I returned, and saw under the sun, that the race is not to the swift, nor the battle to the strong, neither yet bread to the wise, nor yet riches to men of understanding, nor yet favour to men of skill; but time, and chance happeneth to them all. (Ecclesiastes 9:11)

A feast is made for laughter, and wine maketh merry: but money answereth all things (Ecclesiastes 10:19).

And the Lord answered me, and said, write the vision, and make it plain upon tables, that he may run that readeth it. (Habakkuk 2:2)

But I say unto you, that every idle word that men shall speak, they shall give account thereof in the day of judgment. (Matthew 12:36)

For which of you, intending to build a tower, sitteth not down first, and counteth the cost, whether he have sufficient to finish it? (Luke 14:28)

According to the grace of God which is given unto me, as a wise masterbuilder, I have laid the foundation, and another buildeth thereon. But let every man take heed how he buildeth thereupon. (1 Corinthians 3:10)

And whatsoever ye do in word or deed, do all in the name of the Lord Jesus, giving thanks to God and the Father by him. (Colossians 3:17)

And whatsoever ye do, do it heartily, as to the Lord, and not unto men. (Colossians 3:23)

But whoso keepeth his word, in him verily is the love of God perfected: hereby know we that we are in him. (1 John 2:5)

My little children, let us not love in word, neither in tongue; but in deed and in truth. (1 John3:18)

Notes

Notes

Contact James Puckett on the web at:

www.JamesPuckett.com

Additional copies of *When the Boss Is Not Looking* are available from your local bookstore, or at www.JamesPuckett.com or www.bbotw.com

Or contact:

INFINITY PUBLISHING
1094 New DeHaven St. Suite 100
West Conshohocken, PA 19428

www.buybooksontheweb.com

Toll-free (877) BUY BOOK (289-2665)

More books by James Puckett

24/7 Success: Living a Lifetime of Success

Many teenagers may not be concerned with planning their futures. The truth of the matter is, their time may be shorter than they think. Many will waste their time seeking false success rather than focusing on their futures. One day they will turn around and realize they have failed to live life to the fullest. Teenagers need guidance in shaping their futures in order to carve out a life of success.

ISBN 0-7414-3055-X

Denying One's Self in a Selfish World

Life is demanding. Our nature is to first satisfy the flesh. It is not healthy to live a life of selfishness, but always have the needs and concerns of others in mind.

ISBN 0-7414-2610-2

Fighting Fear With Faith: Combating Fear As a Good Soldier

Fear will cause you to give up fighting, loose the fight, or not fight at all. Fear will prevent hope from coming alive. We are told to "fight the good fight of faith." Learn how to stay in the fight and win.

ISBN 0-7414-1956-4

Keeping Your Mind Renewed

You only get one pass for life. The way you think will depend on how you live. Your mind dictates your actions. In order to live a Christian life, your mind must be renewed daily with the Word of God. The Word will prepare you for the struggles you will face on you spiritual journey. Are you prepared?

ISBN 1-59160-054-5

Living Life With Faith In God

It's easy to say we have faith in God when everything id going well. But what happens when you need that prayer answered and it seems God is nowhere to be found? God wants us to have faith in Him when we are patiently waiting.

ISBN 1-931232-24-5

Separation of Christian and Church

Hundreds or even thousands of people who call themselves Christians do not attend Church. Some are seasonal church attendants, while others only attend church when it's convenient to them. The church was established for Christians to assemble, worship, fellowship, and be taught the Word of God.

ISBN 0-7414-1472-4